Cath Senker

THE GREAT NATURE HUNT

BIRDS

W
FRANKLIN WATTS
LONDON•SYDNEY

Franklin Watts

First published in Great Britain in 2016
by The Watts Publishing Group

Copyright © The Watts Publishing Group 2016

Series editor: Sarah Peutrill
Series designer: Matt Lilly
Cover designer: Peter Scoulding
Picture researcher: Kathy Lockley
Illustrations: Andy Elkerton

Dewey number: 598
ISBN 978 1 4451 4523 5

Printed in China

Franklin Watts
An imprint of
Hachette Children's Group
Part of The Watts Publishing Group
Carmelite House
50 Victoria Embankment
London EC4Y 0DZ

An Hachette UK Company

www.hachette.co.uk
www.franklinwatts.co.uk

FSC
www.fsc.org
MIX
Paper from
responsible sources
FSC® C104740

Pic credits: **Dreamstime.com**/Amber Estabrooks 29CR, Ampack 4, Anton Harder 17TR, Eric Gevaert 29CL, Brandon Holmes 23(c), Brian Lambert 13BR, Deepta 23BR, Epstefanov 6BL, Iouri Tomofeev 17BL, Jennifer Thompson 23(e), Lee Amery 17TL, Louise Rivard 24B, Mallios 13TL, Manuel Novo 22, Maxim Blinkov 5, Menno67 23(b), Mikelane45 16T, Nikolay Dimitrov 13C, Operative401 14BL, Sandi Mitchell 19, Spychala Pawel 17TC, Thomas Dobner 14R, Thomas Langlands 17BR, Willi Van Boven 16B. **Istockphoto**/Andy Farrer/lensflairuk 13RC, RyanVincePhotography 25 **Shutterstock.com**/Ainars Aunins 7CR, Aksenova Natalya 21BR, Arturo de Frias contents page, 10CL, Bildagentur Zoonar GmbH 18, Borislav Borisov 29C, Chris Hill 13BL, davemhuntphotography 21BL, Dionisvera 7BR, Eric Isselee 21CL, Erik Mandre contents page, 10CR, Erni 23 (d), (f), Euro Spiders 8, FloridaStock contents page,10TR, Georgios Alexandris 10CR, Glenn Young 28, Gotzila Freedom 13LC, iliuta goean 23(a), Karel Gallas 13BCL, Keneva Photography 10BR, LianeM 6TR, Lucy 20 Menno Schaefer 13BCR, 24TR, Miao Liao 21CR, Michael Woodruff 12, Miroslav Hlavko 6BR, Natalia Davidovich 29BR, Ondrej Prosicky 27, Paul Reeves Photography 6LC, Peppersmint Front cover, Peter Gudella 29TL, Peter Schwarz 7CL, Schankz 7BCL, Sekar B 26, solkahar 14TL, Stefano Garan 10L, taviphoto 7TR, T-gomo 7BL, Tsekhmister 7BCR, Vetapi 7TL, Vishal Shinde 23g, Zhao jian kang 21TR.

Every attempt has been made to clear copyright. Should there be any inadvertent omission please apply to the publisher for rectification.

CAN YOU FIND SIX BIRDS' EGGS HIDDEN ON THE PAGES?

CLARA IS OUT LOOKING AT BIRDS. CAN YOU FIND HER?

There are lots more puzzles in this book. You can solve them by reading the text or by looking closely at the photos. The answers are on page 30.

Contents

The great bird hunt

So you're interested in birds – fantastic! Bird watching, or birding, is a popular pastime and it's easy to get started. This book gives you some basic information about birds and where to find them, along with puzzles and outdoor activities.

Birds live in different kinds of places, so begin exploring in your town or village. Look for a good 'local patch', with a variety of habitats to attract different kinds of birds. An area with a pond or lake, trees and fields is ideal.

Watching a seagull in flight near a lake.

Get prepared

Some basic items will come in handy. You'll need a pair of binoculars that are light and small enough to wear comfortably – compacts might be good. Find a field guide with illustrations of birds and information to help you to identify them. Use a notebook or digital tablet to record details of the birds you see.

Always record details of the birds you see.

Bird watching

Look at this local map. Where would be good places to see birds?

Types of beaks

When you're looking at a bird, examine its beak. It could be long, thin, short or wide. Birds' beaks are adapted to the kind of food they eat.

duck

Warblers feed high in the trees. They have a thin, pointed beak, which is good for picking insects off leaves and twigs.

warbler

Woodpeckers also feed on trees. They have a strong beak for pecking holes to reach insects living under the bark and for breaking nuts.

Mallards are common ducks you'll see on ponds and lakes. The edge of their beak is fringed to strain plants, seeds and small animals from the mud and water.

Birds of prey, such as buzzards and eagles, catch and kill live animals, such as birds, fish and rodents. They have a sharp, hooked beak to attack their victims.

buzzard

woodpecker

6

Beaks and breakfast

Find the right food below for these hungry birds.

woodpecker

duck

eagle

warbler

pond plant

ants

mouse

acorn

Feathers for flying

Feathers grow out of a bird's skin just like hair grows on our heads. Birds' feathers gradually wear out or get damaged. New feathers grow and push out the old ones.

Birds take good care of their feathers so they are fit for flying and insulate their body. They preen to remove dirt and spread preen-gland oil through their feathers to waterproof them. Then they shake to get rid of the dirt, creating a cloud of dust. Birds also bathe regularly in water or dust.

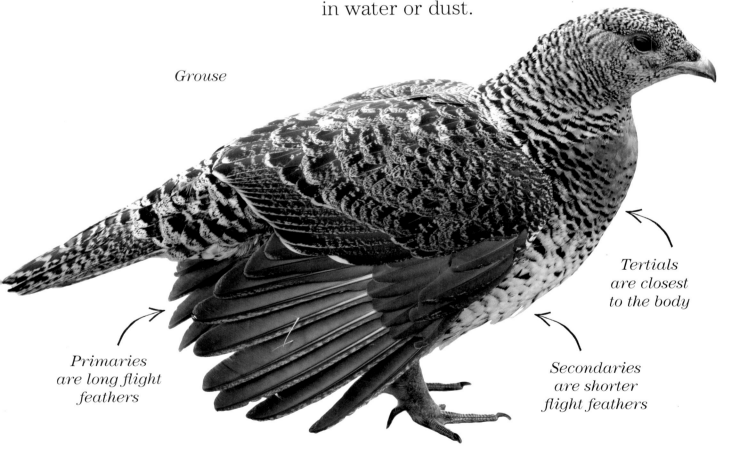

Grouse

Tertials are closest to the body

Primaries are long flight feathers

Secondaries are shorter flight feathers

Feathers overlap so they are streamlined for flight and keep out wind and rain.

Camouflage

Birds' feathers can act as camouflage to hide from predators or prey.

Can you spot six birds in this picture?

THE BIRD HUNT CHALLENGE

Feathers

Wearing gloves, look for feathers in the park and work out which bird they come from.

In flight

Of all the animals, birds are the flying champions. They fly by flapping their wings, steering mainly with their tail. Watching how birds fly helps you identify them.

bald eagle

raven

Eagles and most hawks have long, broad, soaring wings. Their long primary feathers stretch out to catch thermals (upward currents of hot air).

Crows, ravens and blackbirds have elliptical wings, perfect for short bursts of rapid flight. Other birds have high-speed wings for flying extremely fast over long distances – watch ducks, falcons and terns. The fastest flier is the peregrine falcon, which can reach 320 kph – as fast as the highest-speed train!

albatross

gull

Birds with active soaring wings depend more on the wind currents to fly. Their long, narrow wings allow them to soar for a long time. Albatrosses, gannets and gulls have active soaring wings.

tern

peregrine falcon

Which bird?

Identify each bird by its wing type.

a

b

c

d

e

f

THE BIRD HUNT CHALLENGE

Flight

Watch birds to learn the different ways they fly.

Nests for baby birds

These swallows are nesting in a hole in a tree.

Most birds build nests where they lay eggs and often care for their young.

Falcons, owls and many shore birds build simple nests. The plover, a wading bird, makes a scrape nest – a hollow in the ground to stop eggs from rolling away. Falcons often nest in holes in a tree or on cliff ledges.

Lots of birds make more complex nests using small stones, mud, twigs, leaves and other plant fibres. They weave the materials or 'glue' them using mud or spiders' webs. Blackbirds and many other perching birds make cup nests in trees by weaving grass and twigs together. Most elaborate of all are the woven hanging nests built by the weaver birds of Africa.

Find my nest

Which bird uses each nest?

a

b

c

d

THE BIRD HUNT CHALLENGE

Build a nest

Gather natural materials and weave them together or stick them together using mud.

falcon

weaver bird

plover

blackbird

TRY NOT TO DISTURB BIRDS' NESTS AND NEVER TAKE EGGS FROM THEM.

Parks and gardens

This pigeon is nesting in a roof.

How can you attract birds to your garden at home or school? Some birds may come without invitation! Pigeons will nest in a chimney, under roofs and in gutters. Robins love to nest in sheds.

Encourage birds by providing food for them, especially in the cold winter months. Some birds are ground feeders. Ask permission to scatter bird food on the lawn or patio. Look out for thrushes, robins and blackbirds. Sparrows, tits and finches will visit a seed feeder – hang it where cats can't reach it. Tits, nuthatches and woodpeckers will cling on to a mesh feeder to snack on nuts or suet nibbles.

blue tit

great tit

American robin

You can put out a bird bath to provide your visitors with water for drinking and washing.

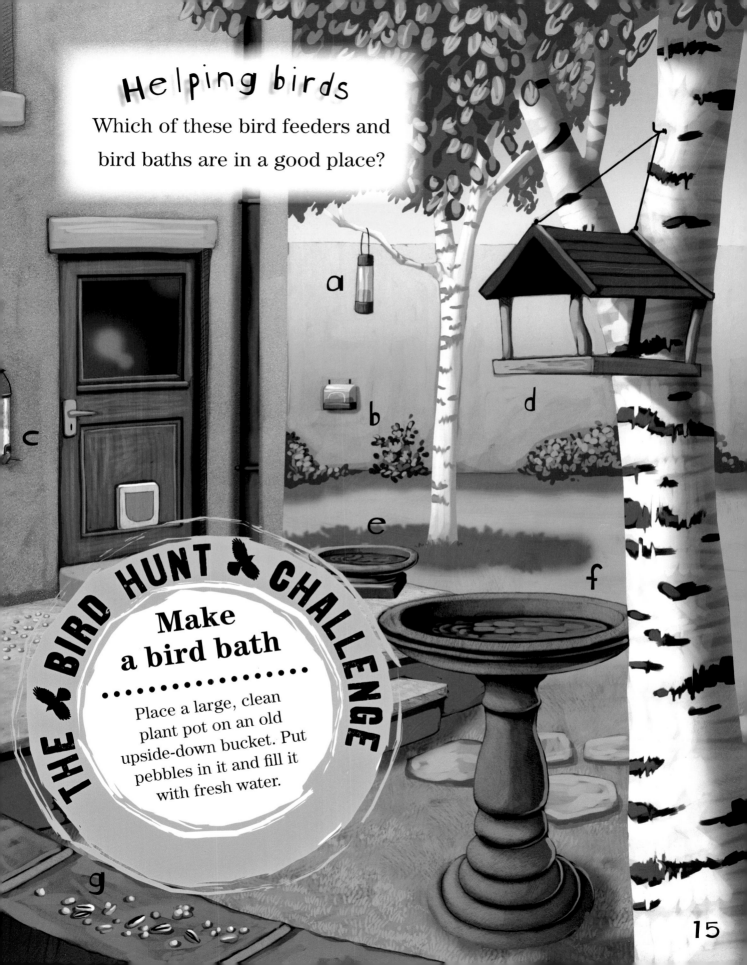

Helping birds

Which of these bird feeders and bird baths are in a good place?

a

b

c

d

e

f

g

THE BIRD HUNT CHALLENGE

Make a bird bath

Place a large, clean plant pot on an old upside-down bucket. Put pebbles in it and fill it with fresh water.

In the countryside

In the countryside, you may spot birds you don't see in the city. Look out for tits, finches, buntings, thrushes and warblers around hedges and trees. In winter, many birds visit bare fields – you may see gulls, wood pigeons, jackdaws, crows, rooks and starlings.

ALWAYS TAKE AN ADULT WITH YOU ON NATURE WALKS AND KEEP TO FOOTPATHS.

Starlings

Barn owl

It's good to learn common bird songs to help you recognise birds – listen to them on the RSPB website. In spring and summer, listen out for the beautiful song of the skylark. In the early morning or late evening, you might hear the screeching of a barn owl.

Silhouette puzzle

Match the bird silhouettes to their pictures.

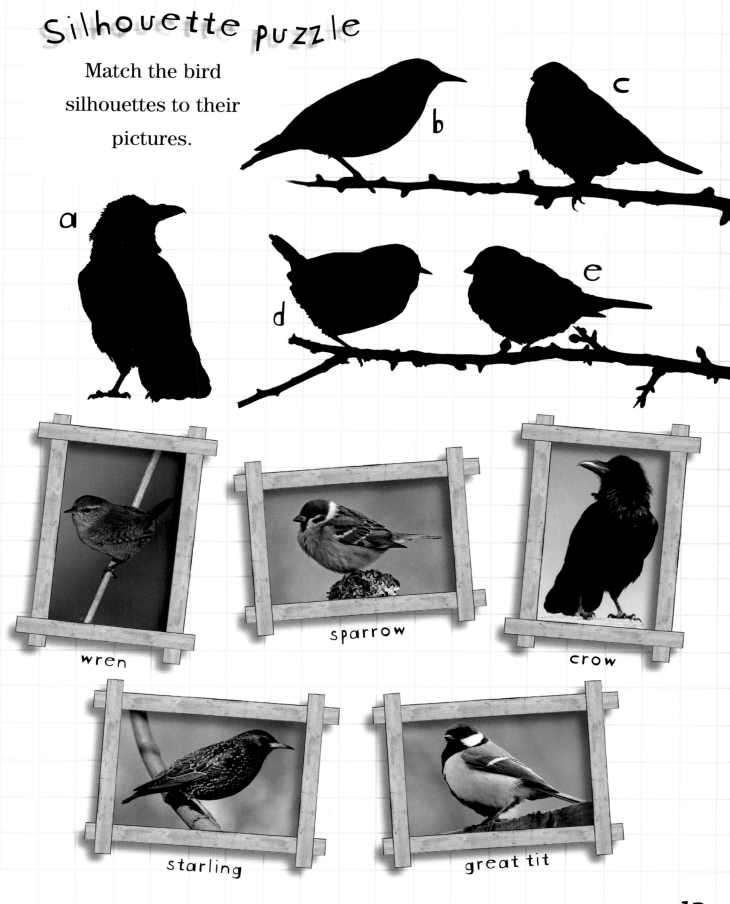

wren

sparrow

crow

starling

great tit

Deep in the woods

Woodlands may have deciduous trees – which lose their leaves in the winter – or coniferous trees, which keep their leaves. They might have both. Deciduous or mixed woodlands are the best for birding.

It can be hard to spot the birds among the leaves. Every so often, stop, wait and watch. Look out for birds moving from branch to branch or from tree to tree. You may see finches, tits or warblers. On tree trunks, woodpeckers or nuthatches might appear.

greenfinch

Draw birds

It's easy to draw birds if
you start with egg shapes.

Can you match the names to the bird shapes?
One name is missing. What do you think it is?

heron   sparrow   owl

Different levels

Scan at different levels: on the
ground, you might spot thrushes and
wrens. Check for sheltered, sunny
patches and clearings out of the wind
– insects cluster here, which provide
food for birds. Birds also gather at
pools of water to drink and wash.

A thrush looks for food on the woodland floor.

Lake visitors

TAKE CARE! LAKE BANKS MAY BE SLIPPERY.

Mallards and Canada geese on a lake.

Lakes and ponds are great places for seeing a variety of birds. Birds feed over, on and under the water. Trees and bushes on the banks of the pond or lake provide food and shelter. Check for warblers and herons feeding at the water's edge. There may be kingfishers perching in trees – look out for them swooping low over the water.

Swifts, swallows, sand martins and house martins fly low over the lake to gobble up insects. Mallards, geese and swans swim on the lake. They duck their heads down to feast on plants, seeds and small animals in the water.

Webbed feet

Have you noticed how swimming birds usually have webbed feet? As they paddle, webbed feet push away more water than feet with separate toes. (You keep your hands together when you swim for the same reason.) When the birds get out of the water, webbed feet allow them to walk easily on mud.

Chinese geese

Whose feet?

These birds have got the wrong feet! Which feet should each bird have?

heron a

kingfisher b

goose c

duck d

21

Where the river joins the sea

At estuaries, the river joins the sea. When the tide goes out, it reveals a stretch of mud with lots of worms, crabs and other invertebrates. They provide plentiful food for birds, including wading birds and others that live near water.

At low tide, keep an eye out for common waders such as sandpipers, curlews, herons and egrets on the seashore. They have long legs for wading through shallow water, and their beaks are adapted for catching and eating fish and invertebrates. Remember to watch for the tide coming in!

golden plovers

Estuary birds

Unscramble the words to find the names of the estuary birds in the pictures.

a naws

b segoo

c lulg

d wulcer

e snadripep

f luckshed

g tormancro

High tide

Visit just before high tide and see if you can identify grebes, ducks, geese, swans, gulls and cormorants swimming in the estuary. Cormorants dive for fish under the water. Look up to discover flocks of birds in the air too. Keep scanning up and down – birds are constantly on the move!

Sand plovers flock over a beach.

At the seaside

On a trip to the seaside, you'll probably notice flocks of gulls. They're not timid, so go up close to get a good view – but watch they don't seize your sandwiches! Beaches and cliffs have big, noisy colonies of puffins, guillemots, razorbills, kittiwakes or gannets – birds that live in groups. Some birds, including gannets, nest on beaches. Make sure you don't disturb them.

A puffin with a mouthful of fish.

Gannets nesting on the shore.

Count the flock

Bird watchers try to estimate the number of birds in a flock. Count a small group of birds. What fraction of the total does this group make up? For example, if it's a sixth, multiply by six to estimate how many birds there are altogether.

Out to sea

Look out to sea with your binoculars and scan for gannets, terns, cormorants, eiders and gulls. Gaze upwards at the cliffs and, if you're lucky, you'll spot peregrines or kestrels.

Peregrine falcons prey on birds such as ducks.

Up in the hills

Hilly habitats are home to several types of birds. When you're hill walking, look for birds perched on fences and boulders. You may see grouse on the ground. Scan the sky for birds of prey soaring over the hillsides, such as eagles, ospreys and buzzards.

bald eagle

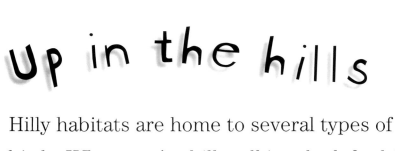

26

Birds of prey are predators. Excellent hunters, they mostly eat small mammals, such as voles and rabbits, as well as birds and fish. They catch them live or find carrion (dead animals). The birds dive extremely fast to catch and kill their prey with their powerful curved talons. Their razor-sharp hooked beak and talons work like a knife and fork, tearing and cutting up food.

Birds of prey, like this goshawk, have keen eyesight and superb hearing.

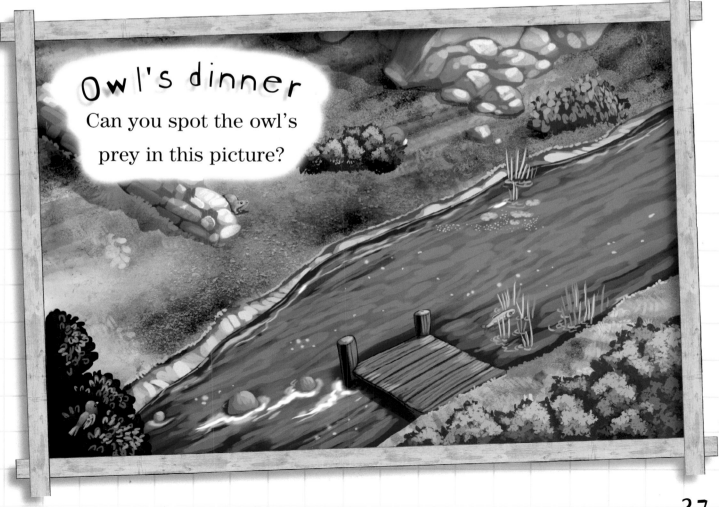

Owl's dinner

Can you spot the owl's prey in this picture?

The birding year

Birds are active all year round. In spring, listen for birdsong and watch birds carrying leaves and twigs to build their nests. Soon, they'll be flying back and forth with food for their hungry babies. Later, you'll see the young birds, which often look different from their parents.

flock of snow geese

Migrants arrive from the South once plants are growing and there are plenty of insects and places to nest. They stay for the summer. At the end of the season, there are fewer insects and many plants are dying, so there's less to eat. Look for swallows, martins, warblers and swifts migrating to warmer areas near the Equator for the winter.

Swallows gather on telegraph lines before migrating from Europe to Africa.

In contrast, many kinds of ducks, geese and wading birds migrate from colder areas to the UK in winter. It's harder to find food in winter, so put out some nuts and seeds and encourage birds to visit.

Bird seasons

Put these pictures from the birding year in order, starting with spring.

a

b

c

d

THE BIRD HUNT CHALLENGE

Nest boxes

Put up a nest box in late winter and see if a bird uses it.

Puzzle answers

5 Bird watching

The riverbanks, woods and fields shown on this map are all good places to spot birds. Birds are all around us so always keep your eyes open to notice them.

7 Beaks and breakfast

woodpecker – acorn
(and seeds and insects)
duck – pond plant
eagle – mouse
warbler – ants

9 Camouflage

11 Which bird?

a – albatross
b – raven
c – peregrine falcon
d – tern
e – bald eagle
f – gull

15 Helping birds

Bird feeders – the bird feeders attached to the tree (**a**, **d**) are in safe places, where birds can feed without coming to harm. The feeder on the wall (**b**) is too low and **c** is too close to the house and to the cat flap.
Bird baths – **f** is in a good place but **e** is too close to the cat flap where the cat could hide and then catch a bird as it bathed.

17 Silhouette puzzle

a – crow
b – starling
c – great tit
d – wren
e – sparrow

19 Draw birds

a – owl
b – sparrow
c – heron
d – The other bird is a duck

13 Find my nest

a – plover
b – weaver bird
c – blackbird
d – falcon

21 Whose feet

heron – d
kingfisher – c
goose – a
duck – b

23 Estuary birds

a – swan
b – goose
c – gull
d – curlew
e – sandpiper
f – shelduck
g – cormorant

25 Count the flock

Five in the highlighted group, which is roughly a sixth of the flock. 5 x 6 = 30 birds in the flock.

27 Owl's dinner

Can you find:
rat
small bird
fish
rabbit

29 Bird seasons

spring – c
summer – b
autumn – d
winter – a

Glossary

adapted For animals, suited to the place they live or the food they eat.

camouflage The way in which an animal's colour or shape matches its surroundings and makes it difficult to see.

colony A group of plants or animals that live together or grow in the same place.

elliptical An oval shape, like an egg.

predator An animal that kills and eats other animals.

preen When a bird cleans itself or makes its feathers smooth with its beak.

prey An animal that is hunted, killed and eaten by another.

rodent A type of mammal such as a rat, mouse or squirrel.

habitat The place where a particular type of animal or plant is normally found.

insulate In an animal, to protect the body, for example, with fur or feathers, to prevent heat from passing through.

invertebrate An animal without a backbone.

migrant A bird or an animal that moves – migrates – from one place to another, according to the season.

streamlined A bird with a smooth, even shape so that it can move quickly and easily through air or water.

talon Long, sharp curved nail on the feet of some birds, especially birds of prey.

wader, or wading bird Any of several different types of bird with long legs that feed in shallow water.

waterproof A substance that does not let water through or that cannot be damaged by water.

Index

Websites

www.birds.cornell.edu
All about birds and how to
identify them.

**http://animals.nationalgeographic.
com/animals/birds**
Identifying birds, bird photos
and a quiz.

**www.naturedetectives.org.uk/
packs/birds.htm**
Activity sheets and videos about
bird life.

**www.rspb.org.ukdiscoverand
enjoynature/families/children**
All about birds and how to help them.

✳

Note to parents and teachers:
Every effort has been made by the Publishers
to ensure that these websites are suitable
for children, that they are of the highest
educational value, and that they contain no
inappropriate or offensive material. However,
because of the nature of the Internet, it is
impossible to guarantee that the contents of
these sites will not be altered. We strongly
advise that Internet access is supervised
by a responsible adult.